The First Book of the
World Health Organization

The First Book of the

World
Health
Organization

by Sam & Beryl Epstein

Illustrated with photographs

79962

FRANKLIN WATTS, INC.
575 Lexington Avenue • New York 22

Library of Congress Catalog Card Number: 63-16914
© Copyright 1964 by Franklin Watts, Inc.
Printed in the United States of America
by Polygraphic Company of America

1 2 3 4 5 6 7 8 9

CONTENTS

FOREWORD

THE WORLD HEALTH ORGANIZATION (WHO) is engaged on a great adventure, that of putting the latest medical knowledge to work in order that all kinds of people in all parts of the world shall be as healthy and happy as possible. WHO helps countries to crusade against disease, and to do what is necessary so that their populations may live in clean and healthy surroundings and have enough nutritious food.

This book, intended for children, will certainly also interest many grown-ups who, in these pages, can accompany some of WHO's doctors as they travel across rough country in jeeps, set up clinics in tents or huts or in the out-of-doors, campaign against disease-carrying insects in jungle villages, or teach nurses, midwives, and sanitarians under the tropical sun. If they wear white coats, it is more likely to be in a research laboratory than in consulting rooms or hospitals.

A book like this can of course tell about only a few of the hundreds of projects that WHO's member states require our organization to undertake, but I hope that it will succeed in opening its readers' eyes to some of the positive benefits that international cooperation can bring to mankind.

Joseph Handler,
Director, Division of Public Information,
World Health Organization, Geneva

vii

The First Book of the
World Health Organization

Four epidemiological intelligence experts at WHO headquarters in Geneva discuss an important message that has just arrived.

WHO/PHOTO BY JEAN MOHR

THE EPIDEMIC THAT DIDN'T HAPPEN

ONE SUMMER DAY IN 1962, an important cable reached the headquarters of WHO, the World Health Organization. The cable had been sent to Epidnations, Geneva, Switzerland. "Epidnations" is the cable address for one branch of WHO — the branch whose full name is the International Quarantine Service.

The cable came from the Ministry of Health in Ottawa, the capital of Canada. It said that a boy who had recently arrived in a suburb of Toronto was ill with smallpox.

Smallpox is one of the most contagious diseases in the world. A smallpox epidemic can cause thousands of deaths.

Epidnations went into immediate action. Reporting epidemics and preventing their spread is its business.

The first step was to obtain the history of the case. Queries produced this information. The smallpox patient, fourteen-year-old James, had been living in Brazil with his parents. A week earlier, on August 11, he and his family had left Brazil for Canada. They flew as far as New York, and James was already sick when their plane landed. His parents believed he had the grippe. After waiting eight hours in New York's Grand Central Station, the family had boarded a northbound train. From Toronto, the next morning, James went on to a suburb of that city to stay with relatives. There doctors first learned that he had smallpox.

James had been on the North American continent for eight days, exposing everyone around him to a deadly disease for which no cure was known. In New York alone, where no cases of smallpox had appeared for fifteen years, he had endangered countless lives. He had imperiled others on his way through Toronto, a city proud of its record of thirty years without a single case of smallpox.

But the experts at Epidnations believed the threatened smallpox epidemic would not occur. There were two chief reasons for their confidence.

1

One reason was that by 1962 several large groups of people — most American schoolchildren, for example — customarily received regular smallpox vaccinations. Many of the people who had been near James would probably not catch his disease because their vaccinations would protect them.

The other reason was that smallpox does not develop inside the human body for ten to fourteen days, and a vaccination given in the early part of that period may prevent the disease's development. If all the people who had been near James could be vaccinated immediately — except those who had recent vaccinations — they might still be protected.

Bulletins on contagious diseases go in and out of Geneva twenty-four hours a day.

WHO PHOTO

There was not a moment to lose, however. The time when the disease might become fully developed in certain people — unless they could be vaccinated first — was only two days away.

With the help of WHO, a vast manhunt began. Its purpose was to track down every person who had been near the sick boy since he left Brazil.

By the next day, Sunday, August 19, that manhunt had reached into three continents.

Some of the seventy-four passengers who had been on the plane with the sick boy had remained in New York, or had gone to some other city in the United States. Others had already flown back to South America. Still others had flown to Europe. Telegrams or telephone calls went out to every one of them, to addresses supplied by the airline or obtained with the help of local police. They were warned of the danger, and told they should be vaccinated.

The crew of the plane was rounded up and checked.

A public health team took three thousand doses of vaccine to the New York airport where James had landed, and vaccinated every employee there — airline hostesses, customs officials, restaurant waitresses, and porters.

Taxi-drivers serving the airport were questioned by police, in a search for the man who had driven James and his family from airport to station.

The three crews of the New York-to-Toronto train were also rounded up and checked.

In the meantime, with the help of newspapers and radio and television stations, public warnings were being issued all over the United States and Canada. Some were directed to the residents of New York and Toronto who might have been near James even for a moment. Others were directed to people who lived in other parts of the continent, but who might have crossed his path.

3

An international passenger shows her smallpox vaccination certificate to a U. S. health inspector. In one year, U. S. inspectors checked 4,383,000 passengers arriving in 32,105 ships and 65,661 planes.

WHO/
PHOTO BY HOMER PAGE

The public warning issued in New York said:

All persons who were in Grand Central Waiting Room between 12:30 and 8:30 P.M. on August 11, or who took New York Central train No. 21, the North Star Limited, that same evening, should be vaccinated by municipal stations or by their own physicians. Members of their families should also be vaccinated.

The people who were nearest to James for the longest time, those other passengers on the Brazil-New York plane, should have been in the least danger. Each one carried a certificate signed by a doctor, stating that its owner had been vaccinated within the past three years. With such certificates they would be allowed to cross international borders, according to WHO regulations enforced by most of the countries in the world.

But the WHO experts knew there was good reason to worry about those passengers. The sick boy himself had been carrying the vaccination certificate required by law. It stated that he had been vaccinated only a few weeks before, in Brazil. If his vaccination had not protected him, the experts realized, there might have been something wrong with the vaccine used in Brazil. Vaccines are seldom faulty; there are WHO standards to which they should conform. But the case of smallpox that James had caught meant that something had gone wrong, somewhere.

Eventually the medical detectives working with WHO learned that the doctor who declared he had vaccinated the boy had not really done so. In the meantime, the hunt for the plane passengers went on.

Monday, August 20, was the day on which the first new smallpox cases might appear, if James had spread the disease to others. Health officials in dozens of offices stayed close to their phones. Monday night passed without any reports of new cases that could be traced back to young James.

Tuesday went by. Still no new cases were reported.

The health centers in New York alone had given thousands of vaccinations by then. Private doctors in the city had given thousands more. Health centers and doctors in other towns were adding to the total. But certain passengers on that Brazil-New York plane had not yet been tracked down. And no one knew how many of the people who walked past James in the station, or sat near him on the train, still lacked vaccinations.

Then Wednesday went by. And Thursday. Still no new cases occurred.

Friday came — the fourteenth day since James had brought smallpox into a region where it had been unknown for so long. If anyone had caught the disease from him, it was almost certain to have shown up already. Nevertheless, no one could say for sure that all danger was past until fourteen full days had gone by.

WHO experts use colored pins to chart outbreaks of smallpox, cholera, plague, and yellow fever. A bulletin published in Geneva sends news of these outbreaks to health officials all over the world.

WHO PHOTO

The hours ticked away. No doctors, no hospitals reported any cases marked by certain telltale symptoms: fever, nausea, pains, and a particular kind of red rash. The day finally ended.

The smallpox scare was over. Thousands of people in New York alone breathed a sigh of relief. They said the story of the epidemic that hadn't happened was a story with a happy ending.

Experts at WHO were saying something different. One of them put it like this. "That kind of story, even with its happy ending, should never have to be told again. Manhunts that reach into three continents cost a great deal of time and money that could be spent in better ways. They could be spent, for example, on a program to rid the world of the danger of smallpox epidemics forever. We have already banished the disease from North America and Europe. We know how to banish it from the rest of the world, too.

"Just vaccinate 80 per cent of the people in every country," he said, "and the job will be done."

6

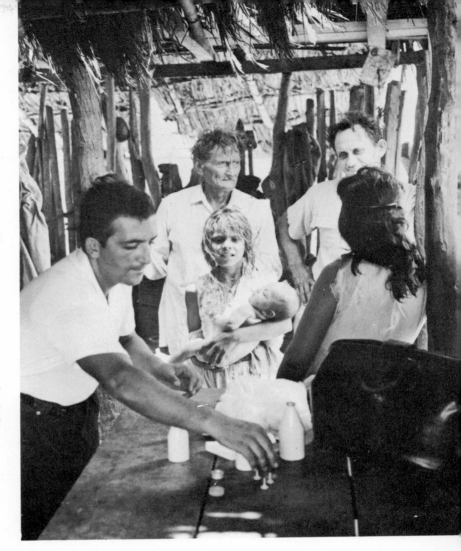

Three generations line up for smallpox vaccinations at a traveling clinic in Colombia.

WHO/
PHOTO BY PAUL ALMASY

The idea of vaccinating eight out of every ten inhabitants of the world still sounds impossible to many people. But WHO has already tackled jobs that sounded equally impossible, and has achieved amazing success.

Take, for example, the job WHO is doing to rid mankind of yaws, a disease known for centuries as "the nightmare of the tropics."

Five-year-old Ede Nwaegbo has yaws.

ONE BOY AND AN ARMY

FIVE-YEAR-OLD EDE NWAEGBO had ugly sores all over his face, and there were sores on his arms and legs, and on his feet. He could scarcely walk. He never smiled. Ede Nwaegbo had yaws.

Many of the other children in his Nigerian village had the same disease. Some of their parents had it too, and because they were unable to work, the fields of their farms had grown back into jungle. Food was scarce.

Nobody in the village, not even the witch doctor, knew any way to cure yaws. Everyone accepted it as a part of life, like the hot sun that beat down on the thatched clay huts year in and year out.

All over Nigeria, and in many other tropical countries all around

8

the globe, there were villages like the one Ede lived in — villages where people suffered from yaws. In 1955, the year Ede was five, he was just one of many millions of people — perhaps fifty million of them altogether — who had those ugly, painful sores, or the crippling deformities that developed later in life.

One day, a big, gray truck drove out of the jungle and stopped in the center of Ede's village. Several men climbed down from the front seat. One of them, who wore a white coat, spoke to Ede's father and some of the other villagers in their own language. He said his name was Doctor Obioha, and that he and the doctors with him had come to the village to cure all the people who had yaws.

"Let me tell you how we shall do it," he said. "First, we shall have to examine everyone in the village. Then we shall give medicine to everyone who is sick. We shall also give medicine to all the members of their families, because some of them may have the disease too, even though it may not show yet."

Someone asked him what kind of medicine he used. He said it was called penicillin.

"Will you help us?" Doctor Obioha asked the men.

Ede's father had never seen a medical doctor before, but he trusted this man. He said he would help.

Finally, all the villagers were lined up. Those who were least afraid of the strangers stood near the head of the line. Only a few people were ahead of Ede and his father.

Soon it was Ede's turn. The doctor looked at his sores and at the sticky yellow pus that ran out of them. He said Ede should be given an injection of penicillin.

Another man showed Ede a sharp needle, and told him that its prick would scarcely hurt. Then he jabbed it into Ede's thigh. Ede jumped. But it was only a tiny prick, and not nearly as painful as Ede's sores.

When everybody in the village had been examined, and many had

9

Left: A doctor arrives in Ede's village in Nigeria.

Above: Ede and his father line up for the doctor's inspection.

received medicine, the doctors packed their equipment into their truck and drove away. They said they would be back soon to make sure their medicine had done its work.

Ede and his mother and father were all amazed at what happened the next day. The yellow pus running from Ede's sores began to dry up. Within a few days many of the sores were covered with scabs that kept growing smaller and smaller.

At the end of the week, some of the sores had disappeared. At the end of ten days, all the sores were gone. Ede's mother and father

Ede is almost cured.

scarcely recognized their son. He smiled all the time. His skin was smooth and clear. He had been cured.

The other villagers who had yaws were cured, too. More people began to work in the fields. Soon there would be more food in the village.

Curing a case of yaws has been called the easiest of medical miracles. The one dose of medicine it requires costs less than the price of an ice-cream cone. It can be given by a medical assistant who has had only brief training.

The antiyaws teams in Indonesia paid special attention to the children.

But eradicating yaws from an entire country is an enormous task, which demands an army of trained people. The disease-fighters in that army must first examine every man, woman, and child in every city, town, village, and farm within the country's boundaries. Then they must treat each victim of yaws, along with those who have been exposed to the disease. And finally, they must reexamine the whole population at least once more, to make certain that their job has been completed.

Only international organizations like WHO and UNICEF (the United Nations Children's Fund) can give countries the help they need to attempt the eradication of the disease. WHO has helped organize antiyaws campaigns in dozens of nations in Africa and South America and among the islands of the Pacific.

In Indonesia alone, antiyaws teams traveled from island to island by small boats until they had examined 34 million people, and treated and cured 5 ½ million.

As a result of WHO's experiment in mass medicine, one of mankind's worst enemies is beginning to disappear from the face of the earth.

HOW WHO OPERATES

ONCE A YEAR, USUALLY IN MAY, men and women from more than a hundred nations and territories come together in a World Health Assembly. They represent the member states, as they are called, of the World Health Organization.

WHO is one of the specialized agencies of the United Nations, but it has more member nations than the UN. Switzerland, for example, which does not belong to the UN, does belong to WHO.

The World Health Assembly usually takes place in Geneva, Switzerland, where WHO has its international headquarters, but it may take place in any country whose government invites it. The fourteenth World Health Assembly, for example, was held in 1961

A World Health Assembly in session.

WHO PHOTO

WHO's executive board meets at least twice a year.

in New Delhi, India. Others have been held in Rome, Mexico City, and Minneapolis.

WHO also has an executive board. It has twenty-four members, each of whom is a health specialist chosen by his own country — one of twenty-four countries which the Assembly selects every three years out of WHO's whole membership. Peru may be among those selected one time; Peru's neighbor, Ecuador, may take her place three years later.

When a board member appears at board meetings, he does not speak on behalf of his country. Instead, he speaks as an individual who has agreed to contribute his knowledge and experience to the cause of world health.

The director general of WHO is a distinguished scientist who serves WHO in much the same way that the secretary-general of the UN serves that organization. He has one of the most important jobs in the world.

The people on his staff range from office boys to world-famous experts in every field of health. They come from almost all the countries that belong to WHO. In the Geneva headquarters there are about seven hundred paid staff members. WHO's total paid staff numbers about 2,500, including men and women at work in the field — on an antiyaws campaign, for example — and in its six regional offices.

Several other specialized agencies of the UN, which work closely with WHO, send observers to each World Health Assembly. Among these are UNICEF, FAO, and TAB. (The second two groups of initials stand for the Food and Agriculture Organization, and the Technical Assistance Board.)

Private organizations, such as the Red Cross, send observers, too. WHO often works closely with the Red Cross. In 1959, for example, when over ten thousand people in Morocco became mysteri-

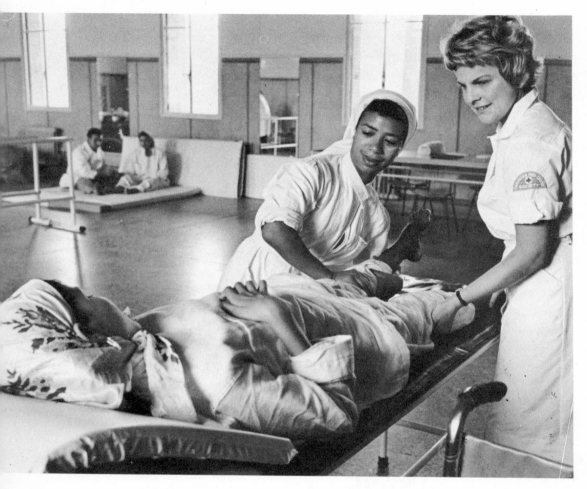

Nurses from sixteen national Red Cross societies assisted Moroccan health workers in helping return paralysis victims to normal living.

WHO/PHOTO BY PHILIP BOUCAS

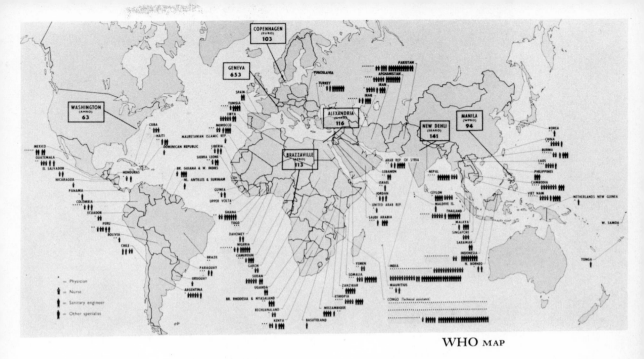

WHO's staff works throughout the world.

ously paralyzed, WHO experts were called on to diagnose their disease and suggest treatment. They found that the paralysis had been caused by poisoned cooking oil, and that special clinics were needed to treat it. WHO experts helped plan and supervise those clinics; the medical teams that operated them came from the Red Cross.

At each World Health Assembly, the director general reports on WHO's work for the past year and suggests a program and budget for the next year. The Assembly members vote on these suggestions, and decide on a budget needed to carry out the next year's work.

Every member state of WHO contributes to its annual budget. Contributions vary according to a country's size and national wealth; the largest, richest nations make the biggest contributions. The regular budget for one recent year (1963) was just over 30 million dollars, or about the cost of two long-range bombers.

Good statistics are the basis of good public health programs.

WHO/
PHOTO BY HOMER PAGE

WHO's Program

WHO's program each year can be divided into two main parts.

One part provides all WHO's member states with certain basic services. The International Quarantine Service is one of these. Another service is WHO's study of health statistics from all member states — statistics on diseases, for example, and causes of death.

Although a number of countries do not yet have accurate health statistics, WHO's study of those that exist has already alerted the world to dangers not fully recognized before. It has showed, for example, that in some countries accidents cause more deaths among children than disease does. Education in accident prevention is now carried out by many of WHO's member countries.

The second important part of WHO's program consists of special projects carried out in various countries, at their request and with their cooperation. The national campaigns against yaws are projects of this kind.

Villagers in El Salvador carry the pipes through which their new water supply will run.

UN PHOTO

In one single year, WHO undertook 825 of these projects of direct assistance to countries. Some projects needed only a single WHO staff member for only a brief period. Others required the services of many WHO experts for many months.

A WHO project may be designed to strengthen the health services of a whole nation — or provide safe drinking water for a single village. In both cases the purpose will be the same: to help a country help itself. WHO's assistance in these projects is therefore mostly of two kinds.

21

WHO fellowships provide nurses' training.

WHO staff members must be able to work in partnership with people of many lands. Here a public health nurse and an Afghan priest are learning to trust each other.

WHO/PHOTO BY MARC RIBOUD

First, WHO may grant fellowships, or scholarships, for advanced study, to a country's health workers. They study abroad, or in some hospital or university in their own region, and then take home what they have learned.

Second, WHO may send experts into a country to work there for a limited period until the country's own health workers are ready to carry on alone.

No project is undertaken by WHO until a request for help is received. WHO does not send its experts into any country unless they have been invited, and unless they will be able to work there in partnership with people of that land. Usually, too, the country itself pays a large share of a project's cost.

23

Leprosy, once believed incurable, is treated today in clinics.

THE STORY OF A WHO PROJECT

MOST WHO PROJECTS COME INTO BEING in about the same way. Take, for example, a project for fighting leprosy in a country we shall call Santa Rosa. (That is not its real name.)

Fighting leprosy was not Santa Rosa's first WHO project. The country had received help from WHO several years earlier, when it first became an independent nation. Then, WHO experts helped plan and organize Santa Rosa's new national department of health. That department began to keep accurate health records — the first such records in that land.

These records showed that Santa Rosa had many leprosy sufferers who were not receiving treatment. The country's health officials knew that leprosy, once considered incurable, could be treated successfully in clinics, and they wished to set up a network of such treatment centers. But only a few doctors and nurses in the country were trained to treat leprosy.

The Santa Rosa government decided to seek WHO's help. It took its problem first to the regional office of WHO, where experts helped draw up a plan for the centers that would be needed. Then that plan was included in the regional program, which had to be approved by the WHO Regional Committee, a committee of representatives of all WHO member states in the region. The regional program then went to WHO headquarters in Geneva. The director general included it in his world program and budget for the following year, which was approved by the World Health Assembly. UNICEF agreed to provide certain medical supplies and equipment that Santa Rosa could not afford. The antileprosy campaign in Santa Rosa was ready to start.

While Santa Rosa set up its clinics at its own expense, two doctors and three nurses from that country were studying abroad on WHO fellowships. Each student spent several months learning about the most modern methods of running an antileprosy campaign. They returned home ready to work with the two WHO experts who had been assigned to the Santa Rosa project.

Together, the WHO experts and the Santa Rosa leprosy team opened the first new clinic and treated the first patients. At the same time, they were training other Santa Rosa doctors and nurses to diagnose and treat leprosy, to keep accurate records of the cases they handled, and to protect the rest of the population from this serious disease.

As soon as Santa Rosa had enough trained people of its own to operate its new leprosy clinics, the WHO project came to an end. From then on, Santa Rosa no longer needed help in that particular field. She was able to help herself. In fact, she soon became a center for the training of workers from other lands, who were sent to Santa Rosa on WHO fellowships to study the best way to treat leprosy patients.

Santa Rosa's antileprosy campaign was an attempt to solve a problem that had troubled her people for centuries. But the next time Santa Rosa asks for help, she may be trying to solve a brand-new health problem — one that didn't exist at all until recently.

The problem might be caused by the development of new industries in the country, or by the introduction of new methods of farming. In a world that changes so rapidly, new health risks are constantly arising, and the people who face them often seek advice and assistance from WHO.

Let's say that the Santa Rosans, like people in many parts of the world today, are irrigating thousands of acres of arid land so that they can grow more food. They are proud of their agricultural progress, but they discover that their new irrigation ditches are excellent breeding places for the tiny snail that carries a disease called bilharziasis (bil-har-zi-a-sis), or snail fever.

A campaign against snail fever can succeed only with the coopera-

Weeding out the water plants on which disease-carrying snails could thrive.

WHO PHOTO

tion of all the people living in the infected region. They must learn to recognize the dangerous snail, and to destroy it, perhaps by weeding out the water plants on which it thrives. WHO experts called in to assist in such a campaign would therefore use various kinds of educational techniques and devices. They might put up posters showing pictures of the snail and the plants it lives on. They might invite the villagers to listen to lectures. They might show a movie especially made to show how the snail breeds, and how to get rid of it.

At the same time, the WHO experts would be using Santa Rosa as a kind of laboratory, where they could work out better ways of curing snail fever, and better ways of killing the snail that spreads it.

ONCE ANY PROJECT IS FINISHED, each WHO expert who took part in it may be given a new assignment. Or, if he is a specialist called in for that one project, he may return to the hospital or health service where he normally works.

In either case, he has new knowledge and experience to take along with him. He shares what he has learned with experts in his own field, and with others who may be able to make use of it. He does this, of course, by talking to the people he works with, but he may do it in other ways, too.

He may write a report, which WHO will publish and distribute as part of its technical publication service. Each year, this service publishes hundreds of books and periodicals in several languages. Doctors and health officers in all parts of the world use these publications to keep up to date with new developments in their field.

Or the expert may pool his knowledge with that of other experts at a technical conference. The many technical conferences that WHO conducts each year are part of still another service that benefits all its members.

WHO publications are printed in many languages.

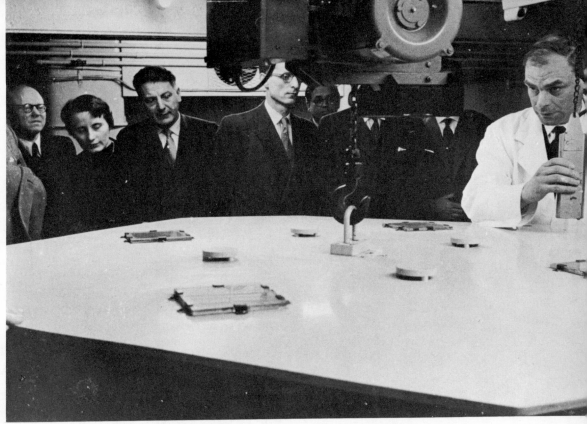

Delegates to a WHO technical conference study the radiation hazards of atomic fission.

Or the specialist may be asked to serve on one of WHO's committees of experts. The members of these committees are drawn from groups, or panels, of the world's leading authorities in various fields. About twenty of the committees meet each year, to collect and discuss all the latest information known to their members.

One group, for example, is made up of experts on cancer research and treatment. Its reports help keep doctors aware of the most modern developments in the fight against this disease. Another is made up of experts in the field of mental health. They meet to talk over the best ways to prevent and treat mental illness, which is recognized

29

Food inspection is one of the jobs of a modern public health service. Here an expert inspects the fish sold in a Congo market, to make sure it is fresh.

WHO/
PHOTO BY HOMER PAGE

as one of the most important health problems in our modern world.

All these committees are called on to advise WHO's director general, when he is planning the organization's program for the coming year.

Thus, all of WHO's various activities — its hundreds of projects and its many services — fit together into its vast year-by-year program for the improvement of the health of the world.

THE IDEAS BEHIND WHO

WHO IS A YOUNG ORGANIZATION. It was born in 1946, when the United Nations invited health experts from its member states to meet together for the first time.

WHO grew out of two ideas.

One of these ideas is that governments can work together to prevent the spread of disease. This kind of international cooperation is over a hundred years old.

The second idea is that every government has a duty to protect the health of the public — that is, of the people it governs. Modern public health services began to take shape only a few generations ago.

Both of those ideas grew out of man's ancient fear of epidemics.

Fighting Disease with Quarantines

In the days before microscopes, when microbes were unknown, the cause of disease was unknown, too. But as people watched a disease spread from house to house and from town to town, they decided it must be contagious: that is, if a healthy person touched a sick person or something that belonged to him, he might "catch" his disease. So, laws were passed in the hope of preventing contagion, and thus preventing epidemics.

One law, for example, forced leprosy victims into prison-like leper houses. Another law forced lepers to carry loudly ringing bells, so that healthy people would be warned to stay out of their way.

In the fourteenth century, Venice passed laws based on this same idea — laws designed to protect Venetians from catching the diseases of foreigners. These laws were called quarantine laws.

Venice was then a powerful city-state with a vast merchant fleet. Every year, hundreds of ships reached her harbor, many from the disease-ridden lands of Asia and Africa. The Venetian laws forced

31

Once lepers carried bells to warn healthy people away.

all these ships to anchor for forty days, at an island outside the city, before they sailed in to unload their passengers and cargoes.

The word "quarantine" means "a period of forty days." At the end of that time, the Venetians believed, a person with a contagious disease would either be cured of it, or dead. A cured person could enter the city without endangering its inhabitants; the corpse of a dead person could be safely buried or burned. A ship's cargo could also be made safe during that period, the Venetians believed, by exposing it to sunlight, or by treating it with smoke.

Most of the countries of Europe followed Venice's example, and set up their own quarantines. Some lasted forty days; some lasted more; some less.

Of course, people had no way of knowing that a rat scuttling down a ship's mooring line might be carrying the microbes that cause bubonic plague. They had no way of knowing that the lice hidden in travelers' clothes might be carrying the microbes that cause typhus.

32

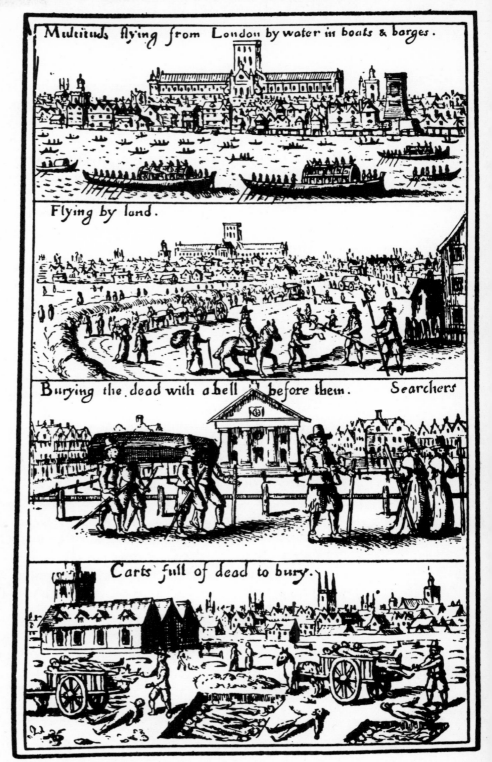

Scenes in London during the Great Plague of 1664.

CLARENDON PRESS, OXFORD

Therefore, people could not understand why their quarantine laws did not prevent epidemics. Governments went on enforcing those laws until the nineteenth century; they knew of no better way to protect public health.

By then, Europe was changing very rapidly. The Industrial Revolution was taking place; factories were springing up to make the things people had made by hand until that time. Farmers flocked into the cities to work in those factories, and cities became overcrowded.

The new factory workers and their families were forced to live huddled together, a dozen people in a single room. Water was scarce and often had to be carried from street-corner pumps. People could not keep their homes or themselves clean. The neighborhoods where they lived became filthy, miserable slums, through which disease spread quickly. During epidemics, corpses piled up so rapidly that cemeteries could not hold them all.

Yet the wealthy and aristocratic people who controlled Europe's governments did nothing. They said that a workman whose home was dirty was simply lazy and shiftless, and did not want to be clean. They saw no connection between the filth of the slums and the diseases that killed so many slum dwellers. They saw no connection between those slum dwellers and themselves.

In 1831, Asian cholera, a disease never before seen in Europe, appeared there. Swiftly it swept through the crowded cities. It struck rich and poor alike, and killed tens of thousands of people.

Seventeen years later, in 1848, cholera again swept over the continent, and again it killed tens of thousands of people. Once more its victims were found in palaces as well as in slums.

Governments became frightened. For the first time, they began to pay serious attention to men like the English lawyer, Edwin Chadwick.

Great bonfires were one of the useless measures taken against cholera before the cause of the disease was known.

Edwin Chadwick, called the father of modern public health services.

Public Health Pioneer

Edwin Chadwick has been called the father of modern public health services. His ideas are common today, but a century ago they were startling.

Chadwick insisted that all English citizens had the right to decent living conditions, just as they had the right to vote. He believed the government should send experts into the slums to improve the living conditions there. He wanted doctors to treat the sick. He wanted engineers to lay pipes that would bring plenty of water to the slum dwellers, and other pipes that would safely carry off their sewage.

Chadwick said England's filthy slums were dangerous to the health of every person living in them, and were equally dangerous to everyone else in the country.

He helped bring about England's first public health laws in 1848. They were not, like the quarantine laws, designed to protect people from diseases brought into the country from outside. Instead, they were meant to protect people from the dangers of bad living conditions inside their own country.

Those pioneering laws helped set the pattern for modern public health services — services that now include sewage disposal; the testing and inspection of water supplies, foods, and drugs to make sure they are not harmful; protection against disease by vaccination; health education, and other sanitation measures.

The First International Health Conference

In the meantime, all over Europe, there was much discussion of the quarantine laws.

Businessmen objected to them, saying that trade suffered when ships and cargoes were held in quarantine for weeks.

Doctors insisted the laws had become more necessary than ever, because with Europe's increasing trade with Asia and Africa, new diseases might be imported from those lands.

Twelve European governments decided that the situation was so serious they must confer about it. This was an important decision. When governments had conferred in the past, the subject had usually been a peace treaty or an alliance for war. Now, for the first time, they were planning to get together to try and work out new and better ways of protecting people's health.

The world's first international health conference took place in Paris in 1851. Some of the delegates were doctors, who argued among themselves over the kind of quarantine laws that would be most useful. The rest of the delegates were diplomats, whose chief desire was to encourage trade and commerce. They too argued among themselves, and with the doctors. That conference, and eight similar ones in the next half century, accomplished very little.

But while those conferences were going on, scientists peering into microscopes were learning that a certain kind of microbe could always be found in a person who had cholera, and that another kind of microbe could be found in a person who had leprosy. The scientists came to realize that those microbes actually caused the diseases, and soon the microscope was helping to find the microbes that cause other diseases, too.

At first, most doctors laughed at the idea that a human being could be killed by creatures so tiny that they had to be seen through a microscope. But the scientists were able to prove they were right, and doctors came to accept the fact that many diseases are caused by microbes.

Here was a turning point in man's age-old fight against disease. From then on, doctors and scientists could carry out a two-pronged attack on the enemy.

One part of the attack aimed at finding microbe-killers — medicines that could destroy disease-causing microbes inside a body.

The other aimed at finding ways to prevent disease germs from entering a human body. In this part of the attack, Chadwick's ideas took on new importance. Now sanitation could be recognized as a powerful weapon against the sicknesses of mankind.

A PIONEER DISEASE-FIGHTER

ONE OF THE FIRST MEN to use sanitation successfully in the field of public health was an American army doctor, William Crawford Gorgas. In 1898, he became the chief health officer of Havana, Cuba.

The United States government had appointed Gorgas to the post when it assumed temporary responsibility for the island of Cuba, after helping the Cubans win their independence from Spain.

Havana had been a bloody battleground during the war that had just ended. The bodies of dead soldiers and horses still lay rotting in the streets; gutters were piled high with garbage and all kinds of filth; people were sick with many diseases — the worst of them, yellow fever.

Neither Gorgas nor anyone else knew where yellow-fever microbes came from, or how they found their way into a human body. But, like most doctors of the time, Gorgas thought that dirt and filth were the breeding places of all the newly discovered disease-causing microbes. He decided that if he could clean up the city of Havana he could rid it of yellow fever.

He put dozens of clean-up squads to work. They carted away dead bodies, shoveled up garbage, swept and whitewashed and disinfected thousands of buildings.

Gorgas clean-up squads ready for work.

PAN-AMERICAN
HEALTH ORGANIZATION

Within a year, Havana became one of the cleanest cities in the world. Its citizens were healthier; certain diseases almost disappeared.

Then Havana was struck by a yellow-fever epidemic that was one of the worst in its history.

Gorgas could not understand his failure, but a few scientists thought they knew the explanation for it. The Cuban doctor, Carlos Finlay, for example, had been insisting for years that yellow-fever microbes were to be found in mosquitoes, and not in dirt — that people got yellow fever from mosquito bites.

Gorgas scoffed at Finlay's idea, and so did Walter Reed, another American army doctor sent to Cuba at about this time. But one of Reed's assistants persuaded him to undertake an experiment with mosquitoes. That experiment, one of the most famous in medical history, proved that yellow-fever microbes did enter a human body on the stinger of a *Stegomyia* mosquito.

Now Gorgas was face-to-face with a new problem in sanitation. To rid Havana of yellow fever, he would have to rid it of the fever-bearing mosquitoes.

When he found that they always laid their eggs in quiet or stagnant water, he ordered his clean-up squads to cover or empty every pool, every jar, every can, or dish, or ditch of water in which mosquitoes could breed.

The Cubans could not understand why their water jars were emptied and their goldfish pools were drained. They stormed angrily into Gorgas' office, and he had to talk to them patiently, day after day, in order to win their cooperation for what he hoped to do.

Weeks went by. The mosquitoes began to disappear, and yellow-fever cases began to disappear, too. In the autumn of 1901, for the first time in Havana's four centuries of history, the city did not have a single case of yellow fever.

In 1902, THE GOVERNMENTS of the republics of North and South America formed the organization that came to be known as the Pan-American Sanitary Bureau. Its purpose was to put into practice, on a hemisphere-wide basis, the kind of disease-control methods Gorgas had used.

A few years later, the governments of Europe formed a similar organization. At first, its chief purpose was to draw up new quarantine regulations based on the new scientific knowledge about disease. Later, it studied many more of the problems that concern modern public health officials.

After World War I, when the League of Nations was established in the hope of maintaining world peace, it formed a health organization at its Geneva headquarters. That health organization became involved with more than the prevention of epidemics and the establishment of quarantine measures. The workers on its staff had begun to understand that if they hoped to reduce the amount of sickness in

Sir Ramaswami Mudaliar of India, President of the UN Economic and Social Council, opened the 1946 meeting which founded the World Health Organization.

UN PHOTO

the world, they would have to improve the conditions responsible for so much of it: poor diet, bad sanitation, lack of decent shelter.

The work of the League's health organization was a great step along the road to today's WHO. After World War II, when the United Nations took the place of the old League of Nations, it quickly called the international health conference that took place in New York in 1946.

To that conference came delegates from sixty-four nations, most of which were facing many serious problems. Cities bombed to rubble had to be rebuilt. Farms and factories destroyed or abandoned had to be made to produce again. Millions of people were homeless. Millions were sick and weak because of years of hunger. Millions had been wounded and needed care. Every national budget was strained by the many demands made upon it.

Yet the representatives of sixty-one nations at the conference signed the WHO constitution — an act that meant their countries expected to become members of the World Health Organization, and expected to contribute funds for its support.

WHO would not be totally new. Its International Quarantine Service would continue the work already started by the health organization of the League of Nations. WHO would simply take over that service, and speed up its program to keep pace with swifter modern travel.

WHO's program in North and South America would be in the hands of the Pan-American Sanitary Bureau, nearly half a century old. The Bureau's headquarters in Washington, D.C., would become one of WHO's six regional offices.

But WHO's goal would be completely new — a goal mankind had never dared aim at before. WHO's constitution describes that goal as "the attainment by all peoples of the highest possible level of health."

The constitution also declares that health is "not merely the ab-

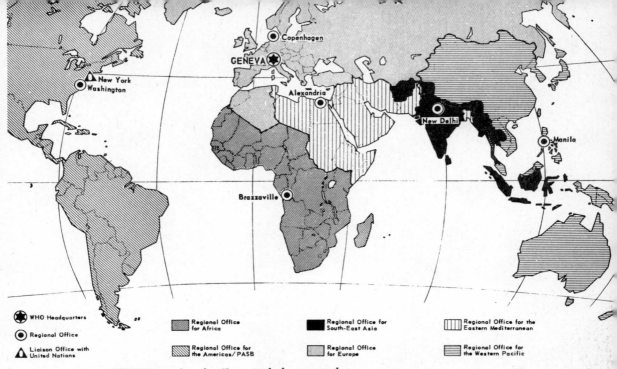

⊛ WHO Headquarters	▨ Regional Office for Africa	■ Regional Office for South-East Asia	▥ Regional Office for the Eastern Mediterranean
◉ Regional Office	▩ Regional Office for the Americas/PASB	▦ Regional Office for Europe	▤ Regional Office for the Western Pacific
△ Liaison Office with United Nations			

WHO's regional offices and the areas they cover.

sence of disease or infirmity." It says that health is "a state of complete physical, mental, and social well-being."

More and more, people had come to believe that a man could not be called healthy simply because he happened to be free of all the ailments that are usually meant when diseases are spoken of — tuberculosis, yellow fever, pneumonia, and many others. A man might not be suffering from a single one of those diseases, and yet might feel so tired or weak or worried that he could not do his best work, or lead a happy and satisfactory life among his family and friends. Such a man, many people had come to believe, needed help just as he would need help if he had pneumonia.

Such a man — all men everywhere — deserved to enjoy "complete physical, mental, and social well-being." That was the decision reached by the founders of WHO. That is the daring goal of this first real World Health Organization.

43

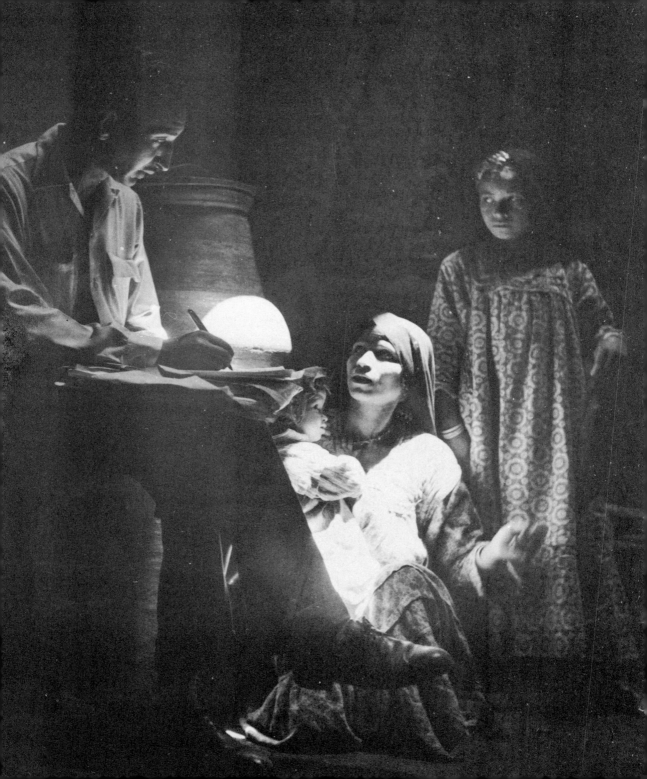

FIRST THINGS FIRST

Delegates to the First World Health Assembly, which met in 1948, faced difficult decisions.

Before them, from dozens of nations, lay requests for urgently needed help.

Some requests were from nations that had hardly any public health services at all. They wanted help of many kinds. In some cases the governments had little idea of the state of health of their people, because it was something they had never bothered about. They had no statistics on how many people died each year, for example, or what they died of. Those nations had to be helped, first of all, to decide what kind of public health services they most needed.

Some nations already knew that they wanted help in setting up the mother-and-child-care programs that are an essential part of most public health programs, and that teach mothers how to care for themselves and their children.

Other nations had mother-and-child-care programs, but wanted WHO's help in expanding their services to include other special

Left: Collecting health statistics is like taking a census.

WHO PHOTO

Right: A WHO expert instructs a young Congolese public health technician in the operation of water-purifying equipment.

WHO/
PHOTO BY HOMER PAGE

An Egyptian nurse teaches mothers how to care for themselves and their children.

WHO PHOTO

groups — school-age children, perhaps, or elderly persons, or those who were physically crippled or mentally ill.

Tropical lands sought WHO's help in ridding their countries of tropical diseases. Industrial countries wanted help in planning attacks on the diseases found most often among factory or mine workers.

There were appeals from countries where people were suffering from malnutrition — the lack of the right kind of food.

There were appeals from countries where people died by the hundreds from those diseases that are usually caused by impure water, lack of proper sewage-disposal systems, and other kinds of poor sanitation.

WHO did not have enough money, or a large enough staff, to respond immediately to all appeals for help. A choice had to be made. Some compromise had to be reached between the world's many needs and WHO's limited abilities to meet them.

Finally the delegates decided to focus their first antidisease campaigns on a few ailments that were widespread and that affected not only the health of people, but their ability to work and improve their own living conditions. Such diseases breed poverty, which in turn breeds more disease. Malaria is one of them. Tuberculosis is another.

The delegates also decided that problems of sanitation, nutrition, and mother-and-child health were among those that must be tackled first. Once those problems were solved in any particular area, that area would be better able to help itself solve its further difficulties.

WHO's staff had already been organized. Now it could start to work.

A WHO expert uses a model village to teach the principles of hygiene and sanitation to young Burmese, who in turn will teach the people of their own villages.

WHO PHOTO

A laboratory technician dissects a mosquito to search for malaria microbes.

WHO/
PHOTO BY ERIC SCHWAB

WHO FIGHTS MALARIA

WHEN WHO DECIDED THAT MALARIA would be one of its first major targets, that disease threatened almost all the inhabitants of the warm, moist regions of the world. It threatened, in other words, about half the world's population.

Only certain drugs could protect a person from catching malaria, or help cure him if he caught it. But the drugs had to be taken every day without fail, year in and year out, or they would be useless. Not many people would take medicine so faithfully; millions of those exposed to malaria, or already suffering from it, could not afford to.

Every year, therefore, malaria struck some 300 million men, women, and children, and killed 3 million of them — most of them children. Those malaria victims who remained alive continued to suffer attacks of severe chills and high fever every few months for years. Each attack lowered a victim's resistance to other diseases, and robbed him of strength and ambition.

Many malaria-infested regions remained largely undeveloped. The disease had made their inhabitants weak and listless. It struck workers brought in from other countries to build improvements like roads and dams. It prevented farmers from cultivating certain rich areas which were infested by the malaria-carrying mosquito.

A single one of these mosquitoes — the female of a genus called *Anopheles* — can infect several persons, in this way. When it stings a malaria victim and sucks up some of his blood, it takes malaria microbes into its digestive system. During the following ten or fifteen days these malaria microbes (or parasites) develop within the insect. At the end of that time, countless newborn malaria microbes are spreading throughout the mosquito's body — many into its stinger, or proboscis. The next time the insect stings a human being, its proboscis injects malaria microbes into that person's bloodstream, thus spreading the disease.

In Iran, an entomologist places a mosquito against a DDT-sprayed wall, to test the killing power of the spray.

WHO/
PHOTO BY PHILIP BOUCAS

WHO's experts had little difficulty agreeing that malaria was a major threat to mankind in almost every part of the world where the *Anopheles* mosquito was found.

They had another reason, however, for deciding to focus their attention on malaria. They would be able to attack it with a weapon more powerful than any which man had been able to use against the disease in the past.

That new weapon was a recently developed chemical, a powder now known all over the world by the three letters, DDT. Its scientific name is dichlorodiphenyltrichloroethane.

DDT is not, of course, a medicine that can be used to cure malaria. It is an insect-killer, or insecticide. It kills by contact; that is, an insect that comes in contact with it will die. And DDT keeps its killing power for months. Scientists had learned that if a surface was sprayed with a DDT mixture, all the mosquitoes that alighted on that surface during the next several months would be killed.

DDT might not be useful, the WHO experts realized, against insects that usually remain in the air. But the *Anopheles* mosquito is usually so heavy after feeding that it rests for a time on some surface only a few feet away from its victim. And the *Anopheles* mosquito usually feeds indoors.

If every surface inside a house were sprayed with DDT, therefore, every mosquito that entered the dwelling would be killed, provided it settled to rest before or after feeding. And if the mosquito had sucked up malaria microbes, it would die before it could transmit the disease.

If one house could be made safe in this way, WHO experts reasoned, they should be able to make a whole region safe from malaria by the same method.

Spraying all the surfaces inside every house, barn, and public building in an entire region would of course be a fantastically big job. It would require tons of DDT. It would need teams of experts trained to carry out the work. But the result would be worth it.

The result would be, first, the death of most of the *Anopheles* in the region who had bitten diseased people and could therefore spread the illness. Within two or three years, the number of people who already had malaria would grow smaller. A few might die. Others would be cured by medicines or by their bodies' natural defenses. Finally, there would be so few cases left that malaria would no longer be a serious menace to the region's health and prosperity. Farms and factories and construction could flourish. People could look forward to a brighter future for themselves and their children.

In Mexico, a new antimalaria team learns how to use insecticide sprayers.

WHO/PHOTO BY MAXINE RUDE

WHO announced that it would send a team of experts to any country willing to launch a campaign against malaria. The team would be prepared to survey the amount of malaria that existed in the country, and would plan the opening attack. The team's members would themselves carry out the first stages of the attack, and at the same time train residents of the country to take over their work. The experts would remain in the country as long as they were needed, until the campaign could be carried on by the people themselves.

By the end of 1949, about a year after the first World Health Assembly, seven teams of WHO experts were already fighting malaria in India, Afghanistan, Pakistan, and Thailand. Other WHO malariologists, or malaria experts, were also lecturing at various schools of medicine, and sending advice by mail to European, Central American, and South American countries where antimalaria projects were going on.

On each WHO team there was at least one malaria expert, an entomologist — or expert on insects — a sanitary engineer trained to destroy mosquito breeding grounds, public health nurses, and technicians trained to use DDT-spraying equipment.

The teams used every possible form of transportation — truck, boat, and helicopter, horseback and muleback, camelback and elephantback. They hacked their way on foot to remote jungle settlements.

An antimalaria team arrives in a Mexican village.

WHO/PHOTO BY ERIC SCHWAB

In some countries, elephants carry the antimalaria spray teams into action.

WHO PHOTO

Every day brought new problems. But the basic problems were always the same. The most difficult one was to win the cooperation of the inhabitants of the villages for the program.

Many malaria sufferers thought chills and fever were a normal part of life; they took their illness for granted. At first, they laughed at the strangers who came into their villages and said they were going to destroy the cause of the disease. But when the strangers walked into houses and began to carry out tables and chairs, the villagers decided they were being invaded by enemies, and they grew furiously angry.

DDT and other sup-
plies are carried on
human backs into the
mountains of Nepal.

WHO/
PHOTO BY ERIC SCHWAB

Their attitude was rooted in ignorance, and ignorance could destroy a whole antimalaria program. It had to be overcome by patient educational campaigns. The importance of fighting the *Anopheles* mosquito had to be understood by everybody, or the fight would certainly be lost.

Slowly, village by village, region by region, the work spread. The number of WHO teams increased. By 1951 it reached twenty-two. Local teams, trained by these experts, were increasing far more rapidly. With enough patience and enough tons of DDT, WHO believed the campaign could be extended until it reached into every malarial region of the world.

Then, in 1951, entomologists working in Greece watched *Anopheles* mosquitoes land on a DDT-sprayed wall, remain there for a time, and fly off, healthy and unharmed.

Worried scientists examined some of these insects that seemed able to survive the insecticide. After long study they proved that certain mosquitoes were immune to DDT, so that the poison had no effect on them at all. The offspring of these mosquitoes were also unaffected by DDT and could therefore be expected to increase rapidly.

A Mexican schoolteacher assists the antimalaria campaign by explaining how paludismo *(malaria) is transmitted.*

WHO PHOTO

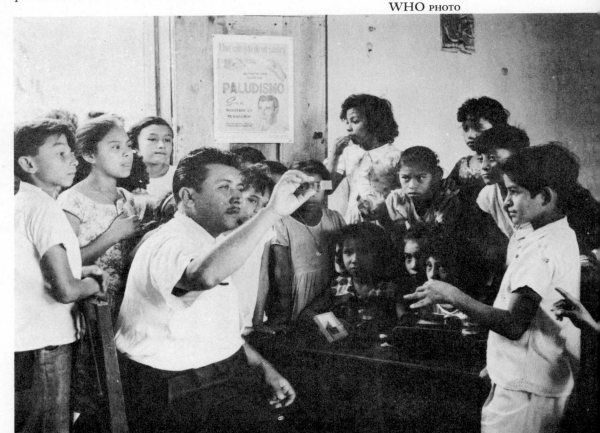

In laboratories, scientists constantly seek new insecticides.

WHO/PHOTO BY HOMER PAGE

DDT could not prevent the spread of malaria in regions where these particular *Anopheles* appeared and flourished.

Other new insecticides had been invented by then. One of them proved able to kill the "resistant" mosquitoes that had turned up in Greece.

But those DDT-immune mosquitoes were only the first sign of serious trouble. Other mosquitoes appeared which proved able to resist some of the newer insecticides, too.

"No matter how many insecticides we invent," entomologists reported, "we will probably always find some mosquitoes which can resist each one."

After years of work and the expenditure of millions of dollars, it seemed possible that WHO's plan to defeat malaria would fail.

WHO's expert committee on malaria refused to admit defeat. It proposed an astounding plan to the World Health Assembly of 1955.

This new plan was based on another surprising incident that had occurred in Greece in 1951. That year, lack of money had forced the Greek government to interrupt its steady spraying program in several parts of the country. Malaria experts, afraid that the disease would instantly flare up with new force in the unsprayed areas, watched them carefully. No epidemic occurred. The several years of spraying that had already gone on had broken the malaria cycle. The number of malaria victims had already dropped so sharply in these areas that the mosquitoes that remained attacked few persons who were diseased. The new cases of malaria that did occur were so few that they could be treated one by one with antimalaria drugs.

That Greek incident, and similar ones elsewhere, seemed to prove that if an area was thoroughly sprayed for several years, it would remain free of disease without further spraying.

The committee therefore recommended that the slow region-by-region campaign be abandoned. It proposed, instead, an immediate attack on malaria wherever it existed — an all-out campaign to wipe

The Army helps plan and carry out Mexico's nationwide anti-malaria eradication campaign.

WHO/
PHOTO BY ERIC SCHWAB

malaria from the earth before insecticide-resistant mosquitoes became too numerous to defeat.

This campaign for eradication of malaria, the committee suggested, would have to be carried out on a scale never before imagined. Its battlefields would be some 150 countries and territories. It would have to be fought at great speed. It would require enormous amounts of knowledge, manpower, supplies, and equipment.

But no other kind of campaign, the committee members said, could defeat malaria.

The Assembly unanimously approved the plan.

The global attack on malaria, which began in 1955, is the biggest public health campaign in history.

The campaign has its own intelligence service. On its staff are entomologists who move ahead of the spray teams to study the mosquitoes of each region. They find the answers to many questions such as these. Do the mosquitoes in this region bite indoors? Do they rest after feeding? Are they resistant to certain insecticides?

Advance scouts also count the number of structures that will have to be sprayed twice a year for at least three years. They calculate the number of spray teams that will be needed to do each job. They estimate the amount of insecticides that will be used. They arrange for transportation to carry men and supplies.

After the scouts come the spray teams, moving from house to house through the territory assigned to them. A supervisor examines each house after it has been sprayed, to make sure that every possible

An inspector in Liberia is ready to mark a house with the date of its fourth DDT spraying.

WHO PHOTO

A malaria spray team awaits the Kurdish nomads crossing this bridge.

WHO PHOTO

Antimalaria drugs have been added to this salt being delivered to a Cambodian village.

WHO/PHOTO BY PAUL ALMASY

resting-place for a mosquito has been coated with poison. When he is certain that a house has been thoroughly sprayed, he checks it off on the list he carries. Then he marks the house with the date of its spraying, and the name of the insecticide used.

Nomadic tribes give the malaria-fighters special problems. In Iran, Iraq, Syria, and Turkey, for example, three million Kurdish nomads wander from country to country with the seasons. WHO teams have set up inspection stations along the route they travel. At those stations, tribesmen are examined and treated for malaria, and their tents and other belongings are sprayed.

63

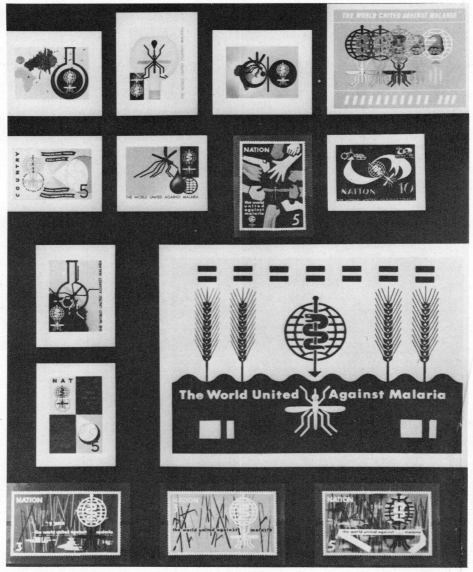

Postage stamps issued by 114 countries helped tell the world about WHO's global antimalaria campaign.

Those nomads, and people living in jungle areas deep inside southeast Asia, Brazil, and Africa, are also given salt to which antimalarial drugs have been added. They might easily forget to take medicine every day, even if it were given to them free. But since they normally salt their food, they now get that medicine regularly with every meal.

Since not every country can afford to pay the high costs of its antimalaria campaign, richer nations — whose own safety depends on wiping out every reservoir of malaria germs — are helping. No country with a malarial climate will be safe from the disease until all other countries have rid themselves of it.

In 1955, when the all-out campaign began, the number of people suffering from malaria was estimated at 250 million. Some six years later, that number had dropped to 140 million, and was still falling every month.

By then, roads and dams were being built in regions where workers on such projects had once collapsed by the hundreds from malaria. By then, too, millions of acres of rich land, once uncultivated, were producing crops to feed the world's ever growing population.

The campaign was making remarkable progress. But WHO's experts would not be satisfied until malaria eradication was complete.

"The job in every region is like rolling a big stone uphill," one expert says. "Getting the stone to within a few inches of the top is not enough. If we fail there — even with a single inch still to go — the stone will roll down again, and all the progress already made could be wiped out."

WHO experts are now confident that the vast campaign will succeed, and that the world can be freed from malaria.

THE STORY BEHIND A STRANGE WORD: KWASHIORKOR

AMONG THE MANY EXPERTS who work with WHO are some who are nutritionists. Their job is to learn what people should eat in order to be healthy, and to help people get enough of the right kind of food. It is nutritionists, for example, who advise us to eat plenty of meat, milk, and eggs, because they know those foods contain a great deal of proteins, the substances necessary for building strong bodies.

A group of WHO nutritionists, meeting with experts from FAO in 1949, decided to study the condition of children in certain African regions where people ate almost none of the protein-rich foods. About fifteen years earlier, an English doctor had reported that the children there suffered from a disease caused by malnutrition — that is, a poor diet. The Africans called the disease kwashiorkor (kwash-ee-OR-kor). A two-man team — one WHO expert and one from FAO — set out to spend two months in Africa, examining children and questioning their parents.

The experts saw many strong, healthy African babies who were growing normally. Those babies were being nursed by their mothers and were getting from their mothers' milk the protein they needed.

But the experts also saw hundreds of children from one to four years old who were sick. Those children had big, swollen bellies. Their arms and legs were as thin as little sticks. They had stopped growing. Many had hair that was faded to a gray or pinkish-yellow color. Many had skin splotched with discolored patches. They whimpered at the slightest touch, but otherwise showed no interest in what went on around them. They were so weak they could not walk.

The experts learned that a child generally became sick at about the time he first began to live on the corn and other starchy foods his parents ate. This time came when his mother stopped nursing him, often because there was a new baby. The African name for the

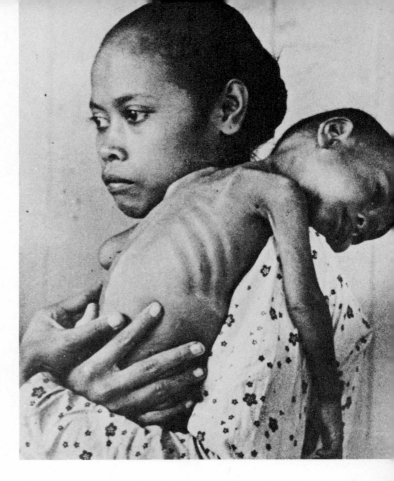

Ill-nourished children are often so weak that they cannot walk, or even sit up.

WHO PHOTO

sickness — the strange word "kwashiorkor" — means "the sickness the old baby gets when the new baby comes."

By the time the two investigators had completed their survey, they knew that kwashiorkor killed thousands of African children each year. They knew that many survivors of the disease remained small and stunted. They knew that children weakened by kwashiorkor often caught other diseases, too — pneumonia and diarrhea, for example — which added to the death toll.

The two experts also had some ideas for fighting the disease. The first thing to do, their report suggested, was to supply African chil-

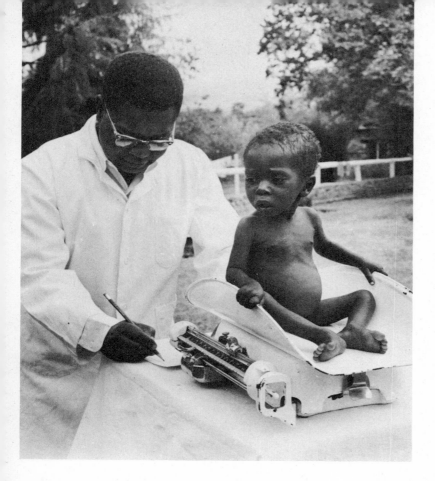

*A three-year-old child
in Africa may weigh
no more than a healthy
eight-month-old baby.*

WHO/
PHOTO BY PAUL ALMASY

dren with some food such as skim milk, which is rich in protein. This would act quickly to fight kwashiorkor and save countless lives.

They also had suggestions for a long-term battle to eliminate the child-killing disease. They recommended that educational campaigns should be started to convince Africans to grow — and use — more protein-rich plant foods, such as peanuts. They suggested that African mothers be taught better methods of preparing food for their children. They urged that a research program be undertaken by medical men, nutritionists, and agriculturists to study the disease from every angle.

The experts' report on their two months in Africa started a great deal of activity. UNICEF began to distribute dried milk to the regions where kwashiorkor was most common, and in dozens of African hospitals babies were saved from death. At the same time, the long-term fight against kwashiorkor began to get under way in laboratories, in clinics, and in agricultural research organizations.

Milk contributed by UNICEF has saved thousands of children's lives.

WHO/PHOTO BY PAUL ALMASY

Many Guatemalan children, like these, live in villages that have no doctors or trained nurses.

WHO/PHOTO BY PAUL ALMASY

In the meantime, nutritionists were asking, Is kwashiorkor only an African disease? They thought it might also be found in other parts of the world where people drank no milk and ate little meat and eggs.

One such place was Central America. In this region, too, there was known to be a great deal of illness and death among young children. A new scientific organization, INCAP — which works closely with WHO — had just been formed there to study the problems of nutrition. (INCAP's full name is the Institute of Nutrition of Central America and Panama.) INCAP investigators began to look for kwashiorkor in Central America.

The INCAP team began its work by studying the health records kept by the various Central American governments — statistics on births, deaths, and causes of death. The records showed a very high death rate for children between the ages of one and four — in some places, forty times higher than the death rate for children of the same age in the United States and Canada. But malnutrition was not given as the cause of death in a single case.

The INCAP investigators trusted the statistics on the number of deaths, but they did not trust the statistics on the causes of death. They knew that few small Central American villages had doctors, or trained nurses, who could accurately diagnose an illness. Therefore, in most cases, the village clerk who kept the records simply asked a mother why her child had died, and wrote down what she told him.

Accordingly, the people from INCAP decided to go up into the mountains and talk to parents in order to collect some firsthand information about the children who had died. For months they traveled from village to village, by car or truck where roads existed, by muleback over mountain trails.

All the mothers they talked to said their children had been given plenty of food, of the same kind the grown-ups of the village ate.

None of the mothers suspected that her child might have died because it had not been properly fed. A great many mothers said their children had died of pneumonia, and a great many more said their children had died because they had "worms" in their stomachs.

The INCAP researchers knew that a child weakened by kwashiorkor could very easily catch pneumonia, and that he was likely to die because his frail body could not resist the disease. They also knew that when a child grew thinner and thinner, even though he was being fed every day, his mother was likely to think the food she gave him was being consumed by "worms" in the child's stomach.

So the investigators asked more questions. They asked how a child had looked, how it had acted, before it died. And then, over and over, they heard about the symptoms that were so well known in Africa: the thin arms and legs, the swollen belly, the discolored skin and hair.

As they went from village to village, the investigators also saw for themselves many young children who had these symptoms. The children were being fed what their parents ate — foods lacking in protein and vitamins. Adults could keep alive on that diet, but it did not contain the elements most necessary for growing bodies.

The INCAP survey proved that kwashiorkor was widespread in Central America as well as in Africa.

In the meantime, in India and other areas, similar surveys were under way. By 1952, kwashiorkor — as doctors everywhere were beginning to call the disease of severe malnutrition — had been unmasked as one of the greatest child-killers in the world.

NEW FOODS FOR BETTER HEALTH

By that same year, 1952, WHO experts were already assisting in an active fight against kwashiorkor and other diseases of malnutrition. It was a fight that could not easily be won.

Nutritionists knew the value of the free supplies of powdered milk that UNICEF was sending to any nation that asked for them. But they also knew why that powdered milk could not be depended on as the only weapon in the battle for better nutrition.

For one thing, powdered milk is expensive. If free supplies of it failed to reach certain needy areas, for any reason, the people in those regions would probably not be able to buy it for themselves.

Another drawback to powdered milk — or any other imported food — is the difficulty of carrying it to every remote mountain or jungle village where protein-rich food for children is scarce.

Still a third drawback, and a very important one, is that people in certain regions believe animal milk to be harmful to children. Mothers in those regions often refuse to give their children milk, even if they can obtain it free, just as some Europeans during and after World War II refused to eat food that was strange to them, even when they were close to starvation.

All over the world, people have this kind of stubborn attitude about food. Everyone believes that certain things are "good to eat," and that other things are "not good to eat."

In places along the coast of Peru, for example, there is enough fish to supply a good protein-rich diet. Adults there eat a great deal of fish, yet mothers do not give it to their children because they are sure it is not good for them. Since the parents cannot afford other protein-rich foods like eggs, butter, or meat, these children suffer from malnutrition.

In Nigeria, the members of one tribe believe that a young child who eats eggs regularly may grow up to be a thief. This belief keeps young children from getting the protein that eggs would give them. Mothers in this same tribe also believe that if children under two years of age are allowed to eat meat, they will develop worms in their stomachs. This protein-rich food is therefore kept from the children at the time when they most need protein.

The experts fighting kwashiorkor realized that food habits and extreme poverty were going to prove the greatest obstacles to providing protein-rich foods for all the people who needed them. To help solve the problem, WHO gave grants of money and expert assistance to three organizations. One was in India. One was in East Africa. The third was INCAP, with its headquarters in Guatemala. In all three regions, experts went to work in much the same way, trying to develop new foods that could be given to young children to keep them healthy.

They knew the foods must have four qualities.

First, of course, they must contain the right amount and the right kind of proteins.

Second, they must be made from ingredients already grown in the regions where the foods would be used. They could not be made from imported products.

Third, they must be produced so cheaply that the poorest family could afford to buy them. Such ingredients as milk, meat, and eggs could probably not be used, because these foods are either unavailable or are very expensive in most places where malnutrition is widespread.

And fourth, the new foods must be acceptable to those who needed them. They would have to look and taste like the foods these people were already eating. The new foods, in other words, would have to fit into the food habits of the people they were intended to help.

In a fine new laboratory built for INCAP by the government of Guatemala, a group of determined scientists began to experiment.

A nutritionist at work in the INCAP laboratory.

WHO PHOTO

They invented one recipe after another. Most of the recipes contained corn, the commonest food of the region. But each one also contained other locally grown fruits, vegetables, or leaves rich in the body-building proteins that corn lacks.

Finally the researchers invented a mixture that seemed promising. It was a yellowish, flourlike powder made mostly of ground corn, cottonseed, yeast, and sorghum grass.

The powder was fed to mice — animals specially undernourished for the test — and they responded quickly. They became plump and sleek and active. Monkeys suffering from acute malnutrition were the next test animals. They too responded to the protein in the mixture, and grew fat and vigorous. Then the INCAP researchers themselves ate some of their new high-protein food, to make sure it could not harm a human being. It passed that test, too.

One day the researchers were ready for the most important test. A tiny boy had been brought into the hospital in Guatemala City.

Guatemalan children drinking Incaparina at school.

He was marked with the ugly signs of advanced kwashiorkor, and seemed almost certain to die. Doctors began to feed him the new high-protein food.

In three weeks the boy had improved so much that the doctors knew he would live. INCAP's scientists had saved his life. The new food they had invented had proved it could be a powerful weapon against the killer of children.

Today the food invented by the INCAP staff is known as Incaparina, or "Incap flour." Its formula, now improved by slight changes, meets all the qualifications the experts had set for themselves.

It can be manufactured and marketed cheaply, at about half the cost of milk. Mixed with water, Incaparina makes a drink that tastes like atole (a-TO-la), a drink popular in Latin America. Incaparina can be served as a cereal. It can be made into a dessert. It can be mixed with the cornmeal used to make tortillas (tor-TEE-yas), the flat, pancake-like bread of Central and South America.

Soon teams were going out into dozens of villages, showing the new food to mothers and schoolteachers, and telling them how it could be used. In one village after another, people were asked to try the food. They tasted it suspiciously. Most of them decided they liked it. They accepted some as a gift. Then, when they discovered how cheap it was and how much it improved the health of their children, they began to buy it regularly.

At the same time, other new foods were being developed by the experts at work in India and Africa. Some contained fish flour. Some were based on coconuts, or peanuts, or soybeans, or other foods already familiar to the people of the regions. In those areas, as in Central America, FAO experts joined the project when the time came to manufacture and market the new food.

Finally, in certain areas, the effects of the new foods could clearly be seen. In Latin America, for example, some of the new generation of children growing up showed that they were going to be taller

A new food made with fish flour gives African children the proteins they need.

WHO/PHOTO BY PAUL ALMASY

than their parents, and taller than their grandparents.

Always in the past the people of that region had generally been short, even though at birth they were about the same size as the average baby born in the United States. They had inherited their small size, it was believed, from their ancestors. Now it began to seem that the children who were getting more protein would grow up to match the average size of adults in the United States and Canada.

Of course, children are not the only ones who benefit from new and better foods. Grown-ups who have good diets are more energetic

In many parts of the world today, a better diet is building a new generation of healthier children.

WHO/
PHOTO BY PAUL ALMASY

and get more done than those who have poor diets. One striking example of this truth occurred in Costa Rica, during the building of the Pan-American Highway.

At first, the workers — who were living chiefly on sugarcane — worked very slowly. A stranger, seeing them on the job, might have thought they were all naturally lazy. Then, as an experiment, a variety of foods was added to their diet. Soon the men were working harder and more steadily. Their section of the highway became famous as the "road that food built."

This example helps explain why the idea has been gaining ground that seeming laziness, and even seeming stupidity, may be "cured" by improving people's diet. To many experts, it now seems likely that the children who are using the new diets in many parts of the world will be more energetic and more intelligent than their parents. No one can even guess how much these children may accomplish for themselves and their nations when they become men and women.

To those children, perhaps — and to all children everywhere — WHO's daring goal will someday seem not so daring, after all. Perhaps these youngsters will grow up to build a world where people will not accept hunger and sickness as a normal part of life. Perhaps, by then, normal living will mean "complete physical, mental, and social well-being" for everyone, everywhere.

INDEX

Not one clicking typewriter, but two — that's the way it is in the Epstein home. Sam and Beryl Epstein worked as a writing team even before their marriage in 1938. Since then, as full-time authors individually or in collaboration, they have written a good-sized shelf of books. Together, they have written as Samuel Epstein and Beryl Williams, Sam and Beryl Epstein, or as a composite character known on some occasions as Adam Allen, on others as Douglas Coe. Individually, Mr. Epstein has written as Martin Colt or Bruce Campbell, and Mrs. Epstein also has soloed, using her maiden name, Beryl Williams. This sounds confusing, but actually it's a simple matter of first-class writing ability, imaginative minds, and those two clicking typewriters.

The Epsteins lived for years in New York City, but they now have a year-round home on the sea-breezy coast of Long Island, where fishing, digging clams, and gardening offer a pleasant change from the literary life.

The Epsteins' books cover a wide range of subjects. Among the titles are *Prehistoric Animals*, *The First Book of Words*, *The First Book of Maps and Globes*, *The First Book of Measurement*, *The First Book of Italy*, *The First Book of Printing*, and *The First Book of Washington, D. C.*

FIRST BOOKS
Complete Check List

Series No.	Quantity	TITLE Author	Listings (A sl L C CS H)	Grade Reading Level
68		**Atlas** C S Hammond & Co	A sl L	3-4
22		**Africa** Hughes	A sl L CS	4-7
140		**Air** Knight	A sl L	4 up
1		**Airplanes** Bendick	A sl L C CS	3-6
76		**American History** Commager	A sl L C CS	4 up
11		**The American Revolution** Morris	A sl L C CS	5 up
158		**Ancient Bible Lands** Robinson	New Publication	
134		**Ancient Egypt** Robinson	A L	4 up
110		**Ancient Greece** Robinson	A L	4 up
150		**Ancient Mesopotamia and Persia** Robinson	A L	4 up
99		**Ancient Rome** Robinson	A L	4 up
73		**The Antarctic** Icenhower	A L C	4-7
77		**Archaeology** Kubie	A sl L C CS	4 up
135		**Architecture** Moore	A sl L	4 up
104		**Astronomy** Grey	A L	4 up
107		**Australia** Kaula	L	4-7
5		**Automobiles** Bendick	A L C CS	3-5
44		**The Ballet** Streatfeild	A sl L CS	4-7
148		**Barbarian Invaders** Sobol	A	5 up
14		**Baseball** Brewster	A sl L C CS	3-5
94		**Basketball** Schiffer	A sl L C	4-8
4		**Bees** Tibbets	A C CS	3-6
98		**Bells** Fletcher	L CS	2-4
18		**Birds** Williamson	A sl L C CS	3-6
2		**Boats** Gossett	A L CS	2-4
101		**Boys' Cooking** Beim	A sl L C CS	4 up
149		**Brazil** Sheppard	A	4 up
43		**Bridges** Peet	A L C CS	3-7
6		**Bugs** Williamson	A sl L C CS H	3-5
153		**California Gold Rush** Havighurst	A L	4-7
65		**Canada** C & M Lineaweaver	A L C	4-6
139		**Cartoons for Kids** Fenner		2-5
111		**Cats** Taber	A sl L C	3-6
54		**Caves** E Hamilton	A sl L C	4-6
45		**Chess** Leeming	A sl L C CS H	5 up
173		**The China Clippers** Rich	New Publication	
146		**Christmas Joy** Wilson	A L	1-3
105		**Civil War Land Battles** Dupuy	A sl L C	5 up
137		**Civil War Naval Actions** Dupuy	A sl L	5 up
29		**Codes and Ciphers** S & B Epstein	A sl L C CS H	3-5
95		**Color** Paschel	A L C CS	5 up
157		**Comunist China** Kinmond	New Publication	
108		**The Congo** McDonnell	L	3-6
9		**Congress** Coy	A sl L C H	5 up
47		**Conservation** F C Smith	A sl L C CS	4-7
85		**The Constitution** Morris	A sl L C CS	5 up
40		**Cotton** Rogers	A L C CS	4-6
13		**Cowboys** Brewster	A sl L C	4 up
10		**Dogs** Taber	A L C	3-5
39		**Dolls** H Hoke	A sl L C CS	1-3
88		**Drawing** Slobodkin	A sl L C	6 up
96		**The Early Settlers** Rich	A sl L C	4-6
81		**The Earth** Sevrey	A L C	5 up
42		**Electricity** S & B Epstein	A sl L C CS	4-8
83		**England** Streatfeild	A L C CS	4-7
26		**Eskimos** Brewster	A sl L C CS	3-5
79		**Fairy Tales** Abell		3 up
25		**Festivals** Reck	A L C	3-6
21		**Firemen** Brewster	A L	3-5
69		**Food** Scheib	A L C CS	3-5
87		**Football** Schiffer	A sl L C	3 up
92		**France** Gottlieb	A sl L C	4-7
61		**Gardening** Kirkus	A sl L C	4-6
122		**Ghana** Lobsenz	A sl L	4-7
155		**Glaciers** Marcus	A L	4 up
60		**Glass** S & B Epstein	A L C CS	3-5
48		**Hawaii** S & B Epstein	A L C CS	4-6
62		**Holidays** Burnett	A L C	3-5
8		**Horses** McMeekin	A sl L C CS	5 up
129		**How to Fix It** Bendick-Berk	A sl L	3 up
143		**Human Senses** Liberty	A sl L	4 up
66		**India** Hahn	L C CS	4-7
103		**The Indian Wars** Morris	A	4 up
15		**Indians (American)** Brewster	A L C CS	2-6
41		**Israel** Kubie	A sl L C CS	4-7
89		**Italy** S & B Epstein	A sl L C CS	4-7
30		**Japan** Mears	A L C CS	4-7
58		**Jazz** Hughes	A L C CS H	7 up
19		**Jokes** Chrystie	A L C CS	3-6
130		**Kings** Newton	L	3-6
172		**Language & How To Use It** Applegate	New Publication	
159		**Legendary Beings** Jacobson	New Publication	
74		**Letter Writing** Jacobson	A L C CS	4-6
160		**Light** Harrison	New Publication	
152		**Machines** Buehr	A	3-6
46		**Magic** Stoddard	A sl L C	3-5
75		**Mammals** Williamson	A sl L C CS H	4 up
90		**Maps and Globes** S & B Epstein	A sl L C CS	4-6
125		**Measurement** S & B Epstein	L	4-6
102		**Medieval Man** Sobol	A sl L	4 up
123		**The Mediterranean** Gottlieb	A L	4-7
63		**Mexico** S & B Epstein	A L C H	4-7
35		**Microbes** Lewis	A sl L C CS H	4 up
116		**Mining** Markun	A L	3-6
51		**Music** Norman	A sl L C CS	3-6
128		**Mythical Beasts** Jacobson	A L	3-5
67		**Mythology** Elgin	A sl L CS	4 up
113		**National Monuments** Lobsenz	A L	3 up
115		**National Parks** Lobsenz	A L	3 up
27		**Negroes** Hughes	A sl L C CS	4 up
154		**Netherlands** Cohn	A	4 up
12		**New England** Rich	A L CS H	4-6
119		**New World Explorers** Rich	A L	4-6
131		**New Zealand** Kaula	A	4 up
72		**Norse Legends** Elgin	L	4-6
16		**Nurses** Elting	A sl L C CS	3-5
133		**Ocean** Epstein	A L	4 up
109		**The Oregon Trail** Havighurst	A L C	3-7
118		**Paintings** Moore	A sl L C	4 up
151		**Pakistan** Bothwell	A L	4 up
84		**The Panama Canal** Markun	A sl L C CS	4 up
50		**Photography** J Hoke	A sl L C CS H	5 up
142		**Physical Fitness** Walsh	A L	4 up
97		**Pioneers** Havighurst		4-8
38		**Plants** Dickinson	A C CS	4 up
37		**Poetry** Peterson	A sl L C CS	3-6
53		**Prehistoric Animals** Dickinson	A sl L C CS	4-7
28		**Presidents** Coy	A L CS	4-6
64		**Printing** S & B Epstein	A sl L C CS H	5 up
114		**Public Libraries** Graham	L	2-4
24		**Puppets** Jagendorf	A L C	3-5
49		**Rhythms** Hughes	A sl L C CS	2-4
55		**Roads** Bothwell	A sl L C CS	3-5
136		**Sailing** M Lineaweaver	A L C CS	8 up
31		**Science Experiments** Wyler	A sl L C	4-6

ALL are supplied in the Watts Guaranteed Library Binding

ALL are in large, clear type

ALL are fully illustrated—many with over 100 pictures, and in color

ALL checked and double-checked for accuracy, authority, and clarity of text

ALL 7¼ x 8¾ size

KEY TO LISTINGS:

A   American Library Association, Booklist

sl Booklist, Small Library Listing

L   Library Journal

C   H. W. Wilson Company, Children's Catalog

CS Child Study Association of America, Books of the Year for Children

H   H. W. Wilson Company, High School Catalog

What they say about
FIRST BOOKS

"Their wide appeal, their broad coverage of varied subject areas, their wide range of significant and timely topics, and their attractive format and illustrations have made them valuable library materials."

MIRIAM PETERSON
Chicago Board of Education

"The format of each book has been superior and the books show that careful attention has been given to design, type, illustration, paper, and binding."

CAROLYN W. FIELD
Philadelphia Public Library

"I have long felt that the FIRST BOOKS developed (by Franklin Watts) were among the important creative contributions made by a publisher in recent decades."

PROF. HAROLD G. SHANE
Indiana University

"I really don't know how we ever ran our school libraries without the FIRST BOOKS!"

ELIZABETH HODGES
Baltimore Board of Education

"In covering a topic thoroughly, these books are like a junior encyclopedia, with an illustrated volume for each subject."

Christian Science Monitor

"Indeed an achievement! The high quality which has been maintained throughout the series is even more remarkable."

RUTH HILL VIGUERS
The Horn Book

"The FIRST BOOKS have made a real contribution in extending the horizons of their readers beyond the interests they knew they had."

JOSETTE FRANK
Child Study Association of America

Write for catalog. Address Dept. Sc

FRANKLIN WATTS, INC. A Division

575 Lexington Avenue   New York 22, N. Y.   of Grolier Incorporated